A Sparrow Stirs its Wings

Praise for A Sparrow Stirs its Wings

Every now and then, when the world seems to be rocked in chaos and people are screaming without listening - vile words and cries for help climbing on top of and over each other - a single voice stands out, and that voice is pure in its truth and stunning in its wisdom.

Rachel Finch, and her debut book, A Sparrow Stirs its Wings, is that voice right now. Turning her heart-breaking abuse into heart wrenching prose, Finch writes her truth and gives her strength to every unnamed victim turned survivor.

A Sparrow Spins Its Wings' is both a hard and a beautiful book to read, the wisdom and the pain contained in these pages demand to be heard and felt long after she puts it all to bed.

There is no voice quite as beautiful as the calm and cool voice of a survivor, an advocate, and a poet, and Rachel Finch is all of these things and so much more.

A Sparrow Stirs Its Wings deserves a much loved place on the bookshelves of survivors across the globe, literature lovers everywhere, and the therapists who are breaking out of the confines of antiquated methods to treat people with breath-taking art therapy.

-Nicole Lyons, *The Lithium Chronicles: Volume One*

A Sparrow Stirs its Wings houses this spirit of fight and flight. Flight not from fear but from the space she has shaped to soar. The structure of the collection reminds me of Alfa's Silent Squall except Finch begins with the girl crossing her heart and hoping to die, walking on eggshells, and ends as a woman who recognises strength and hope in her reflection:

'I did not notice the growth, until I had grown,
I had not seen myself changing, becoming,
until the woman I forged reflected my gaze
and held my stare with no shame.' (Hold the Stare)

In fact, I would even say Finch's sparrow does more than stir its wings – it unfurls them in the morning sun and defies the laws of gravity. This debut collection is more than just honest, beautifully brutal storytelling. Finch has created a collection the reader will feel compelled to return to, time and time again. Moon Breathing makes me fall in love, Heal is the advice I need imprinted on my palm and Still Smouldering never fails to provoke a visceral reaction: 'I was reborn a dragon feasting on the fire in my belly, lit with milk teeth in my mouth'

Finch's voice has found a home, in these pages and in my chest. She touches her readers. She tells the truth and explores hers. She leaves you with the following words:

'You are the smell of rain before it hits the soil.'

And you can't help but believe them.

- Kristiana Reed, *Between The Trees: Poetry and Prose*

'Pieces of me lie scattered in his fingerprints, his voice an echo at the base of my throat and as he nears me, I cross my heart and hope to die.' (He Will Carry Me, As Long A I Will Carry Him)

Amidst the hardships flowing through her veins, Rachel Finch has found salvation from sexual abuse and trauma through her poetry. This piece is just one of the many heart wrenching, soul shattering poems in her debut poetry book A Sparrow Stirs Its Wings. Finch invites her readers to over 120 pieces of her heart & soul, and I can guarantee you will need a box of tissues by your side for this book.

Split into two sections (Part One: Broken Egg Shells/ Part Two: Flight); readers can clearly identify the mood on the pages. Described within her poetic words are hellish moments worded so beautifully that you can't help but to fight back the urge to dive in between the lines and save the girl before danger strikes. Finch's writing is spiritual, delicate, truthful, and at times, heart piercing. There is a cleansing spirit even within the darker portions of the book:

'He thinks the darkness will swallow me whole, but he has forgotten that light burns within me.' (Inner Flame)

The emotions felt are powerful, and paralyzing. Her words are a comforting hand to hold while they take you back to your own tragedies, as she holds you tight through poetry, and comforts you through her ability to be triumphant within turmoil. A mark of a great poet is the ability to make emotional connection with their audience, and Rachel Finch does exactly that.

Abuse is one of the most difficult subjects to write about, talk about, and acknowledge personally, let alone publicly. Finch has a way of bringing abrupt attention to the matter without glorifying it. This subject is trip-wired with fine lines, and she brilliantly dances right over them with a healing warrior goddess mentality and message:

'I spent so long in the dark that the moment the light streamed in, I let it swallow me whole. The beauty was everywhere, is, everywhere. People are so breath-taking. When they let themselves feel, when they choose to house truth on their tongue, when they grow from the pain.' (Growth from Part Two: Flight)

So often we feel ostracized and ashamed because of the terrible things other humans have inflicted upon us. Finch preaches to us to Shed The Shame because we are survivors, not victims; we can learn and grow from the pain, not let it destroy us; we have a choice to harness our power and use it for good, not continue the cycle.

Rachel Finch reminds us that no one can take who we are away from us. We are warriors and she is holding up the eternal flame of righteousness, proudly displaying her battle scars - not for glory – but to share her bravery and reminding us that we are not defined by our tragedies, pain, and suffering. I don't know about you, but I couldn't ask for a better soul to lead me into battle.

-Faye K. Brown, *Beautifully Damaged Things*

Other Books by Rachel Finch

Conversations With My Higher Self

A Sparrow Stirs its Wings

Rachel Finch

INDIE BLU(E)
PUBLISHING

A Sparrow Stirs its Wings
Copyright ©2019 by Rachel Finch

Published in the United States of America by
Indie Blu(e) Publishing

ISBN 978-1-7328000-6-9
Library of Congress Control Number: 2019940904

Editors: Christine E. Ray
Kindra M. Austin

Cover Design: Mitch Green

Dedication

For the women that birthed the strength in me, Celia & Joanna.

For my daughters that carry me in their blood.

For all the women that have walked this path, that are birthing wings.

Acknowledgements

I started writing poetry as a way to deal with the trauma and sexual abuse I experienced as a child. I created a Facebook page, 'Bruised But Not Broken,' and started sharing my past in hopes of both raising awareness and connecting with other survivors. The journey has been incredible.

I have learned that everybody has bruises and that not a single person is broken beyond repair.

As an online community, we have walked our journey of healing together and it has been an honour to do so alongside some of the strongest women I know.

To Tamara Paul - You showed me the support I needed to start this journey and it was your kindness and belief in me that truly began my healing.

To Nicole Lyons - You taught me not to fear my own truth and how to reach in and drag it from my mouth, whole with courage. Not a day goes by that you don't inspire me. Thank you.

To Christine Ray - Thank you for giving me this opportunity. For believing in this book and understanding my story. Thank you for the direction and support. You're an angel in my life.

To My Family - None of this would have been possible without you. You always believed in me, look how far that love carried me. All the way home. I love you all.

To The Poets that Inspire Me - Don't ever stop writing. You are creating powerful ripples in our world and it's an honour to be a part of your truth and your journey with words.

To The Stars That Sent Me Back - You gave me a second chance I didn't know I wanted. Thank you. I will carry this gratitude eternally.

To All My BBNB Followers - Thank you for believing in me, for trusting me and reaching out even when it felt scary. Thank you for walking every step of our healing with me. Warriors that outlived the pain.

Contents

Part One

Broken Eggshells

The Innocence Is Haunting

We were timid girls,
that hadn't known it until
we weren't anymore.
Taught how to keep our lips closed
and our legs open,
too small to know why until the first
hit,
too small to know how to stop the next.
We were a little nest of sparrows,
huddling to keep warm when the dark drew near,
too weak to sing, too fragile to fly.
She said to me, "how can you fear the wolf
if you've never seen his teeth bared?" and I
thought back to the days I would
reach out my hand, with no knowledge of the bite.

Sacred Sister

She lay beside me and held my hand
so with every drum of his voice
she could squeeze life into my palms
and rebirth what had died within my chest.
She lay beside me and whispered sacred verses
once uttered from the witches that cursed our Mothers
and the sound of her singing gave me flight.

Little Girl, Preserved

Little girl preserved.
Her legs numb, heart, desensitized.
Wet grass, sharp, beneath bruised skin.
Unresponsive, wisdom gained.
Little girl, magnified.
Exposed, she balances between worlds.
Consciousness expanding, wings gifted.
She practices worship.
Little girl, illuminated.
She dances to unfold, reveal, evolve.
Yellow daisies tucked beneath tiny toes.
Fragile, the Gods nurture her.
Little girl, grown.
Soldier soul, free.
Kisses of angels stained on pink cheeks.

The Drunk Don't Watch the Clock

Happy hour lasted a little
less than the hour promised,
and I'd count the last seven
minutes down myself,
trying to hold my breath for
the duration, reluctant to
inhale the scent of beer and
vomit creeping up my neck.
I could have sworn I tasted his
breath through my collar bone.
When seven minutes pass and
my hips are still rocking, I
count them down again.

He Will Carry Me, As Long As I Will Carry Him

Pieces of me lie scattered in
his fingerprints,
his voice an echo
at the base of my throat and
as he nears me,
I cross my heart and hope to die.

Divination

At midnight we light the sage,
drizzle honey on our wounds,
listen for his footsteps, and
practice divination.

Moon Chaser

I was vaguely lucid,
and he was high on crystals
when I watched his mood chase
the moon in search of the howl
that lay buried in my bosom.

Sour Doesn't Always Overpower Sweet

She is peaches and cream and
I am the wild, starving.

Courage Became Us

She is soft and willing,
her golden strands entwined
in my fingers and she is
telling me the story of how
courage became us.

I Become the Sun

My being is motionless,
face forced in the soil and I'm
hovering above it again, wings
anchored to the clouds.
I can't see the back of my head
for his and I wonder if I scream
from up here in the wind,
he might hear it.
I can hear the rushing of angels
drawing near and the image
before me disperses into Light.
Fragments of what's real scatter
into matter and I become the Sun.

Our Portrait of Punishment

I am hot and waiting,
drawing constellations in
the bruises on my thighs,
our portrait of punishment for
having pretty faces and heavy hips.

The Prayer Is Alive

The prayer is alive when the sound of it is
in sync with the pounding of my heart,
a background beat
to the screams locked in my gut.
The mother tongue in me is born in the memory of the
women that cried before me and clamped their
teeth down on the pillow so their babies didn't hear.
The prayer is alive when I rise from my body and
float above it,
watching him grab fistfuls of the back of my head and
the angels are singing.
The prayer is alive when Light fills the room
and drags me from the stain between my legs
lifting me to the sky so
the singing of the stars can drown out his grunting.
The prayer is alive when I slam back into my body
and the presence of angels still ripples through me.
I am listening to the sound of the cosmos chanting my
name.

The Power of the Gods

She tells me to recite the curse
of being born a pleasure to
greedy men and I kiss her
broken skin like the power of
the gods resides within my lips
and I can restore her.

Inner Flame

He thinks the darkness will
swallow me whole,
but he has forgotten that light
burns within me.

We Will Love Away the Pain

She calls me Queen of Egypt and
whispers ancient witchcraft into
my mouth and I am already praying
the sorcery loves her through my hands.

And I Am Flying

I am between worlds,
feet on the ground,
head in the clouds,
out of touch with
this life.
Men on my left,
spirits on my right,
feathers bursting
from my back.
My flesh is holy,
housings scars and
I am flying.

Birthing Swans

I never knew strength until
I saw them standing side by
side with grins as wide as
Mount Olympus and a little
voice behind them whispered,
Aphrodite, birth the swans.

Burning Sugar Boiling

She's flushed cheeks and fear,
I am burning sugar boiling.

Painted Thighs

Lay me down and pretend men
of all colours haven't
painted their own shade of
rainbow on my thighs.

The Sound of the Universe Explodes

He tells me I am heaven sent
but he doesn't know the half of it.
Solar systems shatter when my wrists
are bound and within my scream the
sound of the universe explodes.

Girls Are Not For Beating

I take rejection like a winner,
spit the blood from my mouth when you've finished
pounding childhood trauma
into my lungs.
Smile through the bruises, keep your secrets in my
throat, along with your name.
I won't speak you into existence.
My body tapped out, but my spirit's in the ring, I won't go
down.
Fists don't need words to speak, shades of you staining
my cheekbone,
a child's signature.
Numb, I am transparent.
Still, you never knew when to stop.
I used to watch the bubbles of anger form on your lips
and think
maybe if he kissed me this wouldn't hurt.
I was underdeveloped, half your size and yet
it was you who hurt.
Tears falling from your eyes, a little voice in my chest
screaming
"I know"
and I couldn't silence her.
I swallowed your shame and stomached it better than
you could.
I want to spit you out but you've flavoured my tongue
and there are
traces of you in the back of my eyelids.
You thought women were weak, but the same hands
you bound, ground herbs,

whispered sacred words and wiped the salt that you
couldn't carry from your face.
Little boy calm your rage, girls are not for beating,
grow into the skin you hide behind, watch how the
women do it without heaving.
I take rejection like a winner, climbing on the steps I
stumbled on,
kicking them to pieces behind me.
You can't reach me up here, floating with the fireflies.
Bite your tongue, learn release,
I might reach down my hand.

Reaching Stars

There were days we toyed with our
lives just to feel in control of them,
days we spent feet dangling from bridges
telling ourselves if we jumped we'd
reach the stars.

Rebirth

I said,
bury me in December,
so that I might have
time to grieve myself
before summer.

Hope

Hope is a language I
have taught myself
through gritted teeth
with bloody knuckles
and shattered ribs that
refused to let me breathe.

It Was Tragic

It was tragic,
the way we clung
to dreams and longings,
the way they smothered
the trauma with labels
and tried to squeeze
our psyche into straightjackets
too small to bound the inner.
It was tragic,
the way we retreated to our
subconscious and made homes
of the fortresses that
housed the ancient but
remembered.
It was tragic,
the way we sparked up,
chewed Valium to
numb the yesterdays and
mauled at any euphoria
we could claim.

It's Eating At Her

She tells me the fear is in her shadow,
I tell her he's all claws and teeth but
the sharp doesn't damage the tomb.

Pursuing the Gentle

I tell her,
keep the tenderness,
we'll need it someday
to teach the girls we birth
love is not between the thighs
or in the sighs,
but at the tips of gentle fingers.

Rachel Finch

Still Smouldering

I said "What do I do with all this fucking rage?"
and she told me "Swallow it, we will not become them,
turn the pain into flames" and I was reborn a
dragon feasting on the fire in my belly, lit with
milk teeth in my mouth, still smouldering.

Earth Mother Knows

She said,
"When the ground shakes and the
crows circle my crown,
I know you are calling.
When the sky is rumbling and the
wolves are whimpering,
I know the forest is blazing
and my heartbeat is a signal to the
ocean to use her power and drown the damned."

Cursing the Demon

There's selenite in my fist
and voodoo on my lips
and this is how I curse the
demon riding me.

Blood Brothers

We were blood brothers with breasts and bruises.

Let's Eat

She said,
I dare you to be brave and I said
there are dragons in my chest
that want to feast, their flames
a war cry of our purgatory,
let's eat.

Wings

Tender Bones

Slow down, eager hands,
gentle boy with bambi eyes,
I'm not used to tender bones.

Moon Breathing

He looks at her like the moon breathes
in the centre of her chest and she
looks at him like she knows he's right.

Bruised Wings

He's all cut lips and halos
he's all black eyes and bruised wings.

Devotion

I show him devotion when I
bury the blisters beneath
my skin and let him kiss me
where it hurts, where it
cannot be seen.

Moody Lover

She is a moody lover,
hands around her throat,
wet beneath her eyes and
between her thighs.

Ghosts

Ghosts are real and they look like you and me

The Greatest Loss

Things that distract from the pain
- Aligning your face in the stars
- Building constellations in your echo
- Worshipping your ghost

I Was Unforgiving

I was unforgiving when the first hands to love me,
pleased themselves,
I was unforgiving when the first friend to show me the
self,
loved with her hips and not her pulse.
But am I forgiving when her own blood stands before me
and I morph the memory into something beautiful,
for the sake of the baby that came from her womb
and with his innocent eyes looking into mine, I silence
them.
I was unforgiving when I lay there and let her
merge the trauma carried in her muscles, into mine
and told my sister to turn away so the memory didn't
stain
her eyelids, so she didn't feel it.
What was I when I let her lips press down on mine,
still carrying the flavour of her father and I swallowed
both their shame?
How my body wanted to deny her,
but my hands ground down her hips and I needed her to
know,
I knew him too.
I am forgiving when I look back at our prayers, amid the
tears,
that were our words and I still taste her wounds.

Not All Hands

They say this sickness isn't catching,
but we've both got the tremors.
She swallows the pill and I ride mine out,
convulsions to shake off the weight,
the ache, the break.
They say you can't tell when a person's gone mad,
but I know it can be seen lining the pupils of her eyes
and I place secrets in my palms and pray to her breasts
as if I didn't know women could transform hurt to hope
and through the sweat, I see her soul seeping,
and weeping his regret.
They say you can't
hear a heart break, but the sound of her
muffled screams still rings in my ears and I want to go
back
and touch her shoulder blade with the tip of my finger to
remind her, not all hands are rough and uninvited.

Love Doesn't Move

Sometimes people change and all you can do is
watch their lives go to shit.
Sometimes healing hands don't heal,
sometimes they hide in pockets and pinch
themselves to silence the pain.
Sometimes life humbles you and the hurt does nothing
but
sit in your throat and bleed.
Sometimes life reminds you, you are not godlike,
but flesh and bone and rage and heart and mortal.
Sometimes people change, but the love never does,
the love never moves a muscle.

Six-Foot Six-Year-Old

He was a six-foot six-year-old,
his skin, heart, cold as the armour he still wore.
Deep voice booming, heavy gaze looming,
clawing for a control he never felt before.
I watched him suck the life from her lungs
and fill his own with a power born from her fear
and he sickened me.
I traced the cut on her skin with a shaky hand
and she flinched.
And she flinched.
She pulled away from soft hands, she knew
and I watched him smirk.
I tasted the vomit in my mouth all the way from
my stomach and gagged on the flavour of the blood
seeping from my heart up to my tongue.
I poured honey on her wounds, thick to hide the
shame and I swallowed blame, his and my own for the
days I watched him shrink her and said nothing.
He was a six foot, six year old,
internal bruising lining the under layer of his body
and he kicked her in the playground that their boys
played tag in and I chased them so he didn't have to.
I chased them so when they looked back they'd
remember
my smile running after them and their mother's
face toward the sky, her back to him,
her back to his knife, back to his wounds that
were still living.
He was a six-foot six-year-old,
and we mothered him.
We offered love to an orphan that had never felt warmth

but he did not thaw.
Now I fan the fire to keep the heat and intertwine it in their nervous system so they never feel the cold they were born into.
So she never remembers the frost.

Archangels

I told her a lie in his voice
and she clawed his name out of
my mouth with the strength
of a thousand men and a couple
archangels too and my throat
was raw with shock and fresh air.

There Was No Fucking Hero

Even the heathens used to suck on their Mama's titty.
There was a time the addicts cried
for milk and that was enough.
Those babies grew with love in their hearts and
still the world beat them down.
People, beat them down.
I've watched everyone I've ever loved reach out for
comfort.
I've watched them all reach for a damn fix too.
But I don't get mad.
You know why I don't get mad?
Because those babies grew into children,
suffered at the hands of men claiming to be human and
they've been gagging on trauma ever since.
But no-one's there to pat their backs.
Couldn't soothe the colic,
can't help heave the vomit.
There is no support system.
Just little girls hiding behind big tits and long eyelashes,
painting smiles onto their faces,
as if foundation hides the streak of tears,
we know it doesn't.
Little boys, bruised, looking up at men that fathered
them and then taught them everything love isn't,
through their fists.
Rape, carried behind their eyelids,
beatings still living beneath their skin.
There was no fucking hero.
Just small people, reaching for a bottle,
reaching for a titty that's dried up,
a fucking hand to hold that can't be found,

because Jesus, to touch them,
would be to risk the plague.
And you walk by.
I have watched these people crumble.
I have watched them stomach grief,
living with a bad taste on their tongue,
struggling to spit the pain from their lungs and
I have watched them fight.
The shame in their chests,
the weight on their shoulders,
their broken hearts barely beating.
They were anything but weak.
And you think you're better than them,
because you carry your pain in your pockets and
you can handle the heavy that weighed them down/
You did not live their path.
I guess I do get mad,
when their bodies convulse,
when they throw up as much as they choked down,
when they laugh amidst the agony of overdose.
But not with them.
With those of you that think you're a fucking
gift to the planet,
but can't be a gift to a brother.
The addicts don't disgust me,
humanity does.

Nostalgia

Sometimes I am nothing but a little girl,
nostalgic for better days, behind me.
Sometimes my words are fierce, my tongue sharp,
my heart like stone.
I am a growing compilation of all the girls
and women I have been.
I am whole in my multitudes.

Rotten Heart Chakras

And I wanted her to know,
until she knew.
I was alone in a
dark place that smelt of
rotten heart chakras and
burning petals and it was
quiet when the sky stopped
singing.
I wanted her to know I grew
my hair to hide the tattoo
of the God that betrayed me
on the back of my neck and
that the carpet burns on my knees
were from praying and not
fucking like she thought.
I wanted her to know the
rage that made a home in
my stomach, starved my hunger
and forced me to spit at
the shooting stars that span
around me after each blow.
I wanted her to know despite
the bitter on my tongue, I
still looked up and had the
audacity to be grateful.

To Unravel Him

He left lesions on my flesh and I have sewn the
torture whispered from his lips into my skin.
To unravel him.

Soul Ruler

She claims the stars spinning around her head, her
crown.
Her throne, built within her spine,
crafted by their mistakes and her knowings.
With wisdom carved into her bones and a river of truth
flowing through her blood,
she raises the kingdom in her chest and becomes the
Queen of her own empire.
She is the ruler of her soul.

Spine of Steel

She taught me regret
is a flavour
that I can gag on
when I remember my
spine was still steel
before I knew it.

Salt Water

There are many beautiful ships that lie wrecked.
Their stories submerged beneath waves and intertwined
with coral.
I am a beautiful wreck too.
With other people's secrets buried in my bones,
their sins knotted in my nervous system.
I wonder if salt water stings the oceans' wounds,
the way it stings my own.

Ancestral Wounds

She's braiding my hair and
chanting and I am learning
strange is beautiful when the
wounds of a woman's ancestors
are living in the spaces
behind her eyelids.

The Wounded

Because it's the wounded who go home wise.

Part Two

Flight

Rachel Finch

Hollow

I can see the babies that met
their end in my womb
in my peripheral vision and they are
smiling.
I scatter rose petals into the ocean
in their memory
and see Cherubs dancing on the horizon.

Out of Body

I thought he could break me
until I was broken and still
thinking outside of my body.

Flavour of Light

I kissed the sky and all I could taste was
the flavour of the stars.
I kissed the sky and all I could taste was
light, light, light.

Shooting Stars

Freedom was a foreign word until
I rose above my corpse and had
shooting stars for heartstrings
and asteroids for eyes.

Without This Purpose

I am hovering in paradise,
where nothing bruises and the
stars are telling me secrets.
The moon remembers mine and
says "Become me" and every phase
of existence enters the centre
of all I am.
I say "Let me stay..." but I already
know, the planets will collide
without this purpose.

Heaven

Heaven stared at my betrayal,
and granted me devotion.

The Night Sky Speaks

Little Starchild,
don't forget the promise.

Astral

My soul has crossed dimensions
to enter this space.
I am from a distant star and
sometimes little sparks fly from
the crowns of the people
beside me in battle and I recognise
the same constellations in their eyes.

Still, He Stays

The unravelling
is
what remains.

A Sparrow Stirs its Wings

In my dreams the blackbirds are singing and
in my chest a sparrow stirs its wings.

Divine Timing

I'm not about to pussyfoot my way around healing,
it's ugly, it's messy and
I've never been more ready.

Flight

Birthing wings from the pit of my stomach,
I'll fight, I will take flight.

Clairaudience

Fear tasted sweet on my tongue when
I stopped crying for the Gods and started
listening for them instead.

Luminescence

I am moonberries and quartz
and I am luminescent.

I Am

I am both the flame and
the water that douses the fire

Birthing Bravery

Little girl's that know they can survive,
grow into women that mould strength into their being.
Little girls that fight for their life grow into women
that will fight for more than survival.
Little girls that fight demons,
grow into women that laugh at adversity and exude
courage.
Little girls that meet with fear,
grow into women that do not have any.

Lava Veins

It is always dormant,
this lava in my veins.

Growth

I spent so long in the dark that
the moment the light streamed in,
I let it swallow me whole.
The beauty was everywhere,
is, everywhere.
People are so breath-taking.
When they let themselves feel,
when they choose to house truth on their tongue,
when they grow from the pain.

Shed the Shame

We are what we think we are,
so we gotta monitor that shit.
Shed the shame.

Holding Peace

There's grown men hiding in the chests of our sons and
when the time comes little boys will become husband's
and father's to Queens.
Don't let them carry war in the space that could hold
peace.

Yet Angels Weep

We are taught that tears make us weak and we hide
behind that illusion,
stifling emotions, burying pain.
We are more determined to feel a dry burn behind our
eyelids than the
softness of a tear that brings release.
We are told that strength does not cry,
yet angels weep.

Soul Signature

Become aware of your own energy,
it is the signature of your soul.

Breathe

Walk barefoot in the forest.
Ground yourself with nature.
Let the roots of the Earth flow through you and
breathe.
You are One with the planet, the moon, the sun, the
stars.
Let those powerful energies reignite you from within.

Healing Powers

Don't underestimate the healing power of these three
things,
Music
The Ocean
Stars.

Build

Your soul will never die and never fail you,
Build with it.

Love Is a Rescue

He knows I love him by the way I
trace the patterns on his skin
as if the salt doesn't
burn my fingertips,
as if my bones haven't memorized each scar,
as if my blood doesn't carry the sound of his
hope, for him.

Wrath

I am a storm of silence.
The beat of your own heart racing,
the only sound you'll hear
when you feel my thunder through the soles
of your feet and know
the wrath is coming.

Stars, Speaking

I've been talking to the stars since I was five years old,
I've got a hand to hold.

My Own Definition

I am not,
will not,
could not be,
defined by you.

You Are All Glory

You think you're a piece of shit,
because someone else treated you as if you were.
You think you don't matter
'cause no one ever took the time, to show you, you do.
You put yourself down because those closest to you,
put you down first and you hide because others have
preferred to see you hidden.
Enough.
You are all glory.
You are the Light in your eyes when the Moon glares
above you.
You are the smell of rain before it hits the soil.
You are the ethereal wings beating behind your back
and
your voice is the whisper of an angel.
You have the blood of a bear and the same bite too.
Unclamp your jaw.
Having the mentality of a piece of shit will hinder your
growth.
With the claws of your Spirit, scratch back your power.
You've forgotten how to hunt,
now is the time to remember.
You are not a piece of shit.

Heal

If you need to heal,
find water and stars.

Seashells

And when she finally speaks,
you will hear the sound of seashells.

Still, I Singe

I've got a lot to say, but I rarely say it.
Words stick in my throat along with the lies they spoke,
kissing their way into my mouth,
down my windpipe and into my lungs.
It is in the centre of my chest that the greatest part
of me lies and I have kept her hidden.
My heart is an iceberg begging to thaw, but it seems the
only
heat I can handle is that which beams from my fingertips
and singes all that try to know me.

The Gift

Life is snatching the breath from my lungs again,
wisdom hiding within my temple.
I am the temple.
I know some people that didn't feel this way until
they grew old and died,
but I've done that shit.
Without the body, the spirit soars
and I'm already flying.
There is nothing more beautiful than the struggle,
than the breath, than the rest, than the rebirth.
To be human is a gift.

Bluebird

He does not give life to your tongue,
sing your song bluebird.

Fear Is Dead

If he strikes you, baby,
let it light the fire
in the heart of every woman
and shoot flames into the
underworld to show
the devil fear is dead.

Little Red

Little Red Riding Hood didn't stay little
and she's coming for the wolves.

For Survivors

Put down the pain.
The shame is not yours to carry.

Listen

I'm still whispering to myself, talking my way through the
horror,
"You're not a little girl anymore, you can do this."
And as I do, I question how many other little girls are still
clawing their way up from the battlefield within
and I make the conscious decision to raise my voice.
"You're not a little girl anymore, you can do this!"

What It Means To Be Brave

Climbing out of the tomb you buried yourself in when
you decided you were no longer enough
Flying higher than your fear and choosing every day to
believe in yourself and all that you deserve
Staring at your own reflection and recognising the child
that's always been within you
Honouring her

Mantra

You
Are
Not
What
They
Did
To
You

Climb

You've spent so long building walls,
let them be the structure on which you climb.

Furious

As a child, I was afraid.
As an adolescent I was sad.
As a woman, I am furious.

Self-Acceptance

I used to think,
why am I so sensitive.
Now I think,
wow, what a privilege.

Rachel Finch

She Is Not For the Taking

And when I birthed a daughter,
a bonfire singed my womb and
my femininity screamed,
She is not for the taking.

Burst

Your soul demands growth, be ready to expand.

Rachel Finch

Hovering

I can be seen, spanning mountain peaks and
hovering between flares and shadows.

I Keep My Memories in a Castle

I keep my memories in a castle
in the back of my mind and when
I need a little motivation I
look back at the damage still
living in the walls and I let
the haunting reignite the flames
of the fire that kept me warm
throughout the freeze.

Spectrum of Colour

My knees have known bruises,
a spectrum of colour, staining my skin as a reminder.
Pigments of who I am, altered at their hands.
Fists clenched to strike, imprint.
Each stain a bolt, a language seeping into my essence,
teaching.
My ribs have known bruises,
painted, I am every female ancestor face first in the dirt.
My throat has known bruises,
I never felt so transparent as I did wearing lesions
beneath a high collar.
Fading, my shell returns,
burying the real wounds beneath it.
But I am wiser.
Healed, I am every female ancestor, facing towards the
sun.

The Wound Was the Portal

Instead of rebandaging each wound,
I performed open heart surgery and
faced every fear I had been running from.
The wound was the portal that led to every
answer I had been seeking.

Rachel Finch

Herbs & A Smooth Rhythm

Give me low lighting.
Give me herbs and a smooth rhythm.
Give me crystals I can balance on my temple and
a love that can't be found in any religion.
Give me the little things that help soothe my soul and
I'll give you a woman, whole.

Breathing Stardust

Every flutter of your eyelashes creates ripples in this
Universe
and every time you exhale, you breathe a stardust all of
its own into existence.

The Growl

Healing is chaotic.
It takes courage and faith in our own strength.
When we are afraid to feel, we block our ability to heal.
Our wounds may be gaping, but there is beauty in the
struggle,
beauty in each scar, power in growing through distress.
Healing will crash down those walls we built and
force us to rummage around in our own soul.
Healing is violent and intense.
We cannot rush recovery, but we can learn to face our
fears and
fall in love with the truth of who we are.
Our bodies may be delicate, but our spirit is fierce.
Unleash the growl.

Divine Selves

In order to know our divine selves,
we must create a sacred space for reflection.
This is how we meet our depth,
this is how we gain our wisdom.

Self-Love

Magic happens when you learn to love who you are.

Who You Are

Empower yourself with
Honesty
Resilience
Compassion
Determination
and the
Freedom
to be who you are

Otherworldly

I can show you heaven, if you can handle hell.

Tides

Healing comes in waves.

Mother Tongue

I am a woman,
channelling rage from my belly,
birthing light in the hollow of my throat.
You cannot silence the mother tongue when
it is truth.

Aligning

I replaced fear with slow breath.
I replaced anxiety with gratitude and my whole being
aligned.

Co-Existence

I am the wound,
the healer and
the healing.

The Ground Is Not Made For Your Gaze, Warrior

It doesn't matter what kind of day you've had, listen to
me.
Sit up straight, push those shoulders back,
who taught you to slump like your spine isn't the core of
your strength?
The ground is not made for your gaze, warrior, head
high.
You are not the sum of your experiences.
You are the wisdom that grew from the birth of each and
every wound.
You carry mountains in your back muscles.
you were made to stand.
Now rise.
The battlefield is not quiet, beside you,
an army of hearts and swords.
Fear nothing my love, your power is already within you.

Birthing the Healer

The healer must acknowledge that some people are
unaware of what needs healing in their lives
or how to cure their own emotional bruises.
The healer must show people their own magic and
enchantment so that they recover each and every
time they face trauma in the future.
The healer must work on the wound that bleeds today,
whilst also teaching that it is safe to
open old lesions and softly restitch them with the sorcery
coursing through our veins.
The healer knows the only way to heal, is to teach the
wounded of their own healing powers.

Needing Nothing

She is not afraid to be lonely.
Solitude has been a lifelong friend,
Connection is important to her
and she'll fight for strong bonds.
But she doesn't need them to thrive.

Warrior That Outlived the Pain

She taught herself strength.
Led her own recovery and made the conscious decision
to heal from the trauma.
She trusted the visions she saw in her mind's eye and
dedicated the future to the spirit within her.
Survivor of abuse.
Warrior that outlived the pain.

My Name

My name is not in the suffering,
My name is in the healing.

 Rachel Finch

I'll Crown You Queen

Tell me that he raped you
and my own womb will feel it.
Tell me you're still standing
and I'll crown you Queen.

I Remain Unshaken

Any man would have crumbled,
but I am not a man,
and I remain unshaken.

Rachel Finch

The Warrior Is Woman

What is a warrior, with no armour?
What is a warrior, with no sword or shield?
What is a warrior, with no army,
but fight?
The warrior is woman.

Hold the Stare

I did not notice the growth, until I had grown,
I had not seen myself changing, becoming,
until the woman I forged reflected my gaze
and held my stare with no shame.

About the Author

Rachel is a UK based writer that originally started using poetry as a way to accurately express herself after a number of traumatic experiences in her young life. She is the founder of the online community Bruised But Not Broken which was started with the purpose to raise awareness of abuse and trauma and to provide a place of comfort and support throughout the healing process. She firmly believes that it was with the support of this community that she was able to recover from sexual abuse. Rachel is mother to four young children and dedicates her time to her family and to guiding others on their own healing journey.

You can connect with Rachel on Facebook and WordPress under Bruised But Not Broken.

Made in the USA
Columbia, SC
07 July 2019